MW00882469

Dedicated to my Dad

Jackie Davidson
And all the coal and shale miners
Who worked in such horiffic places
Thank you for our warm fireside

This is a work of fiction
Any resemblance to real person, living or
dead,
Is purely coincidental

Just Another Wednesday

1

A soft breeze played about Nancy's hair as she stood in the warm sunshine waiting for the green bus into town. She was alone at the stop, and this pleased her, for she had no desire for idle chit chat today. Her trip into town was not something she cared to discuss with anyone else. Nancy knew she had the reputation among the village women as being stand offish, but it was just the way she was. She always felt uncomfortable at the way the other women seemed quite at ease discussing their personal lives with each other, her thoughts were that personal lives were private and that was how she liked to keep hers.

Opening her best handbag she removed the soft blue leather purse that Peter had given her for Christmas. It was an expensive item but he had insisted she was worth every penny, including the one that was taped to the inside flap so the purse would never be empty. Glancing at the penny a soft smile moved round Nancy's face. She was so fortunate in her choice of husband, she loved Peter dearly and both of them adored their outgoing little daughter beyond measure.

As the old green double-decker bus rolled to a stop and Nancy boarded to the friendly greeting of the conductress, the woman at number six felt a pinch of envy.

Grace Graham was looking out at the quiet street that ran along the front of the row of miner's cottages where she lived with her husband Alex and their three boys. Like most miner's rows Braeside had no gardens attached to the front. There was a large allotment area on the far side of the village which most of the men, and even a few women, took advantage of to grow their own vegetables. Potatoes, turnips and carrots, along with cabbages and brussel sprouts were the most popular. Peas were also planted but many were lost to raiding children who enjoy the fresh peas straight from the pods. Anyone who tried to grow strawberries was thought to be mad.

Today was a lovely bright day. Yes, it was a perfect day for a stroll in the park, or a ramble up the hills. Grace thought wistfully. Or, there again, for hanging out the large wash that was lying in the wicker basket in the washhouse. What with baby Tom's nappies, and Alex's very dirty pit clothes it had been a busy morning.

Grace hoped that this was a taste of the weather to come, then the spring of Nineteen Fifty would be something to look forward to. 'Perhaps I'll put young Thomas in his pram and meet the boys after school.' she thought, 'then we can take a walk up the pit brae and on out to Mile End farm and pick up some of Annie's new fresh eggs. Alex was fond of scrambled egg on his pit piece. 'Nice and moist,' he always said, ' when your mouth is dry from coal dust.'

Grace had just popped in from the wash house to check on baby Thomas, no worries there, he was sleeping soundly in his cot which was alongside the high double bed. The bed where his father lay snoring, catching up from a hard night shift down the local pit.

Gazing from the window she had observed Nancy Martin getting on the bus. 'Swanning off to meet her friends, I expect,' were the thoughts that ran through her head. 'All right for some; one wee girl, a man who worships her, and a mother to take up the slack. Not like me, two boys in school and one in the pram.' "Stop it," Grace admonished herself. Everyone knew that Nancy would give her eye teeth for another child. It just didn't seem to be happening.

Smiling at herself she took another look at the baby, then, closing the door quietly, made her way through the back kitchen and out to the drying green.

*****

The wash house, and drying green were shared by all the families in the row. Each day, except Sunday of course, four different women would take it in turns to use the deep chipped sinks and the copper boiler that was housed in the far corner. It was a roster strictly adhered to, and it was a matter of luck if you got a good breezy drying day, or one when the rain made it impossible to hang things outside. When it was wet, as it often was, the women had to drape everything on the pulley, and sometimes on the wooden horse placed round the fire.

Today, Wednesday, Grace was second in line to Nancy, who had made an early start leaving her plenty time to go into town. Her washing was already flapping gently in the westerly breeze, and her mother had promised to bring the clothes in if rain threatened, or if she was late getting home.

Stringing her line up from pole to pole, Grace smiled inwardly, remembering the time she, and her sister Jean, had cut a large chunk from their mother's line to use as a skipping rope. When mother found her line too short to reach the poles she had threatened to whip them. It never happened of course, but they were kept indoors after school for the rest of the week, and were given more than normal work to do around the house. Truth to tell, Grace thought mother was glad when the week was up, and she could chase them out from under her feet. That skipping rope lasted for years. It was used by many children in the street, all chanting the rhymes, and queuing up for their turn. It was later confiscated by Mr O'Brien, the headmaster of the primary school, when the Chapman boys used it to tie up a couple of younger girls, while playing cowboys and Indians

While Grace was hanging out her washing, Maggie at number seven, was preparing John's breakfast. It was John's habit to have a bit of toast and a cup of tea when he rose in the morning. At around 10:30am he had his breakfast with bacon, eggs, and fried bread. Sometimes it varied but only by a pork sausage or some black pudding. Once, Maggie had added a couple of mushrooms, but John discarded them as "to fancy." He was a man who liked his food plain.

Their daughter Nancy was always telling them that fried food was unhealthy, to which John would reply, "Good food never fattened a pig." Maggie was unsure what he meant by this, but knew he enjoyed his breakfast and didn't see anything wrong in what they ate. Many a family would be glad of what went on their table.

The bright light in John's life was his seven year old granddaughter Elsie. Elsie was Nancy and Peter's only child, and it looked like she would remain so. When John had broached the subject of more grandchildren, Maggie promptly told to mind his own business, and he had gone off with his nose in a sling.

Elsie was a grand wee domino player, her grandad had taught her well, and now she gave him a challenging game. Today she was expected at her grandparent's house after school, as Nancy had gone into town, and John had the dominos lying at hand, ready to set up when she arrived.

His arthritis wasn't too bad today; it was always a bit less painful when the weather was warmer. Some days it was so bad he found it hard to move from his chair. Luckily he had a good wife who did not complain, although it often made John feel guilty that he caused Maggie extra work.

Maggie, on the other hand, did not look on it as extra work, he was her husband and it was her duty to do her best for him, as he had always done his best for her. It was not only a duty, but a labour of love. John had worked hard at the pit face for many years to make a decent wage for his wife and family, and, unlike some other men, never kept her short. So now, when his body was worn done, and his breath came in rasps, Maggie cosseted him, and fed him fried breakfasts, against all good advice, for her instinct told her he would not see many more winters.

*****

Grace had finished pegging out her washing, and looked in again on the baby. He was as sound as before, and Alex likewise. Grace gazed fondly at this big ungainly husband of hers. He was working the nightshift for the second week in a row. Peter Martin had asked him to swap shifts as Nancy hadn't been too well lately, and Peter was loath to leave her alone at night. Of course Alex had agreed. It was not unusual for the men to do this and help each other out.

Quietly closing the door Grace made her way back to the washhouse.

Young Isobel Ford was third in line. Isobel who was in her last month of pregnancy with her first baby was having a hard time leaning over the tub with the scrubbing board when Grace came in through the heavy old door. 'For goodness sake, girl, give over,' she admonished the young girl, ' I don't want to be delivering your baby on the wash house floor.' 'I know, Grace,' murmured Isobel, ' but mother is coming for my lying in and I don't want her thinking I keep a dirty house.' "I'm sure she will think no such thing,' replied Grace, coaxing her to sit down on an old basket chair that lay among other junk in the corner, while she took over.

As Grace started on Isobel's sheets Ellen Chapman came in. Ellen was fourth in line for the washhouse. She always went fourth although the other three took turns at first, second, and third. Rolling up her sleeves, she helped Grace with the sheets, turning the heavy mangle as Grace fed them in. Isobel, rubbing her aching back, was very grateful for the help of her two friends as she would never have managed the mangle on her own.

The three women chatted of everyday things, and of course the talk got round to the coming baby, and all the nappies Isobel would have to wash once he, or she, arrived.

Ellen had a lot of experience in washing nappies, six bairns in less than eight years. William Chapman had a lot to answer for. Everyone knew, or thought they knew, what poor Ellen had to put up with. His drinking, his womanizing, and, some said, his violent behaviour towards his uncomplaining wife.

The other women in the village tried to lighten her load without appearing to pity her. That would never do. Grace, Isobel, and even Nancy left bits of worn soap and washing soda by the scrubbing board, and with Ellen being fourth in line very often there was a good full boiler already warmed with her neighbour's coal. Most miners' wives had plenty coal, but Chappie was not above selling his allowance for beer money.

The van men from the local co-op store were also heroes in this respect. Davie the butcher always made sure that the soup bones Ellen bought had more than the required amount of meat still clinging to them. Her half pound of mince got another dollop after it had been weighed and the odd sausage found its way into her meagre purchases. Then there was Jimmy the baker who accidentally squashed some bread so it was not fit to sell, Ellen's brood did not mind squashed bread, it went well with the overripe bananas from Ben McCabe the fruit man.

Grace liked the woman for her fortitude. She had never heard Ellen say a bad word against Chappie. Sometimes Grace herself would make excuses for Chappie. Her parents had lived next door to the Chapmans when Grace and her sister were young girls. Mr Chapman was a drunk, an ugly one at that, and his wife not much better. The rows that emanated from that house were, at times, quite violent. Many a time the Chapman boys had sat in the Stewart's kitchen while Grace's mum fed them bread and jam, and pretended not to hear the commotion next door.

There were times the boys would sit outside McKenna's pub until one or other of their parents were shamed enough to come out, and throw them the price of a bag of chips. They had to learn to survive on their wits, these boys. It was sad that Chappie, the oldest and most handsome had gone the way of his father, they say the apple does not fall far from the tree. Peaty, the second son, was in jail now, but the two younger ones had joined the army. There was hope for them at least.

There was a time Grace had found herself attracted to Chappie, with his good looks, and silver tongue. Thankfully Alex Graham came into her life and all thoughts of the silver tongued young fly- by-night fled.

When Grace left school she had gone to work as a dairymaid on Joe McKenzie's farm. Alex was a farm hand, a few years older than the new dairymaid, but before long the two started walking out together.

After they were married and their second son was on the way Alex realised that the small wage he earned on the farm was not enough to care for a growing family, so reluctantly he signed on at the pit. This secured them a pit house, cheap coal, and an improvement in wages.

A good strong worker Alex had worked his way up the ladder a little, and Grace had come to terms with her man going down the shaft each day. After the first few weeks, she did not allow herself to think of the cage or the conditions Alex worked in. It was the life they had, like many others, and you just had to make the best of it.

Ellen knew the efforts her neighbours applied to make her life a little bit easier, and she was grateful, even more grateful that it was done in such a way so not to make her feel bad. She tried to repay their kindness in some small way. Like this morning, helping Isobel with her washing, and often taking care of neighbour's children when the need arose. No one worried about leaving their children with Ellen, she was known to be a good mother. Her children might wear hand me downs and live on meagre fare, but they were well loved, and a friendly little bunch, showing none of their fathers bad temper. Not for them the sort of mother Chappie had lived with. The boys and the little girls seemed to accept their life without question but Ellen knew that her eldest, Agnes, was beginning to wonder and notice a lot more of what was going on in her home.

Often, Maggie Wilson, at number seven, would ask Ellen to run an errand for her. Mrs Wilson's daughter, Nancy, was a bit of an enigma. She had been in Ellen's class at the big school, and even then had thought herself better than the rest of the girls. That sort of attitude was certainly not encouraged by her mother, and Joe, her younger brother was one of the nicest, easy going, lads in the row, if not the entire village.

Placing her wash in the large boiling copper Ellen returned to the green to help Isobel, and Grace finish pegging Isobel's sheets on the line. Baby Nell was sound asleep in her pram by the kitchen window; the two small girls were playing in a pile of sand tipped on the edge of the green. Ellen's three other children were in school.

Mr O'Brien, the head teacher, without permission from the authorities, had allowed four year old David to attend the infant's class. This was another kindness that made Ellen's life just a wee bit easier.

Looking at her daughters playing contentedly in the muck Ellen tried to picture their little faces when they saw their lunch today. Jimmy had 'accidentally' dropped a whole fruit loaf on the floor of the van. "Would Ellen kindly give it to old John's dog?" He had asked, as he placed it beside the brown loaf and threepence worth of tea bread on her tray. Ellen knew full well that the fruit loaf had never been anywhere near the floor of the van. Aye, people were kind if you just let them be. So why did it make her feel so sad. She didn't understand why she felt so down, she should be over the moon.

All last week she had lived with the abject fear that she was once again pregnant. This morning she woke to realise it wasn't so. Her relief had been great. Chappie had warned her he wanted no more children, as if she made them all by herself. She also knew her children had more than one little half sibling running around the outlying villages. Chappie of course took no responsibility for these children. On one occasion an irate husband had beaten him so badly that Ellen thought he would need to go to the hospital, but Dr Craig had managed to patch him up, and advised him to mend his ways. Once, after treating Ellen for yet another household accident, the Dr had tentatively suggested that she may be better off without Chappie.

'And where he thought I might go with six babies,' Ellen wondered. Even her own mother, while feeling sorry for her girl, was of the opinion 'you made your bed, you lie in it.' That, of course was the start of the problem.

When young Ellen Gillespie had fallen for the undoubted charms of handsome William Chapman, she found herself lying in a bed in no time flat. When she told her parents she was pregnant; her mother cried, her father raged, and her brothers threatened to beat the hell out of Chappie if he did not marry her. Only her sister May had tried to talk her out of it 'Don't marry him,' she had pleaded 'you will regret it for the rest of your life.' But Ellen didn't listen, and three months before Agnes was born she married William Richard Chapman in the registry office in the city.

Not for her the white flowing gown of her dreams, a plain everyday frock with a small spray of violets given to her by loyal May, who stood witness along with Chappie's younger brother, apart from the bride and groom, the only two people at her wedding. Now look at her, eight years on, an old woman before her time. Chappie didn't look so good either, the drinking was taking its toll on his good looks, but he still had the patter and the women he met in pubs still fell for it.

*****

Nancy sat with her ankles neatly crossed as a lady should. The waiting room was cool and comfortable with a good selection of current magazines. The blonde receptionist had taken the referral letter from Dr Craig and asked Nancy her details. A large blue file with her name boldly printed on the front cover now lay on the desk.

Nancy had never been prone to nervousness but today her stomach was tightly clenched, if such a thing is possible. She was here at Dr Craig's behest. He had referred her to Dr Melville who was a leading expert in woman's troubles, and woman's troubles Nancy had. Her cycle had always been erratic but it was not a subject openly talked about.

In the seven years after Elsie's birth there had been many times she thought she might be pregnant, a hope dispelled after a few days. On three occasions however she had indeed been expecting a baby only to lose it at around ten weeks. The last time was only a couple of weeks ago.

'Spontaneous abortion,' was the expression the Dr used. Nancy hated these words even if the term was technically correct. No one, other than Peter, her mother, and the Dr knew about the pregnancies and that was how she wanted it to stay. It was nobody's business and she did not want anyone's pity, to Nancy that would have been unbearable.

She was here to see if the specialist could find a reason why she could not hold on to her babies. She had experienced no problems with Elsie, falling for her ten months after marriage, an easy enough nine months, and, although not an easy birth, nothing to dramatic. At least not according to some, the stories she had heard of some births would make your hair curl.

Pete would love a son, what man wouldn't. And dad, he had hinted often enough that Elsie could do with a wee brother. Well maybe if her brother Joe got a move on he might be able to give dad the grandson he so wanted, what's more, one with the Wilson name.

Joe had been seeing a lot of the new infant teacher up at the wee school. Alice Tod was her name; she lodged with Mr O'Brien and his wife at their cottage in the village proper. Nancy liked the look of her; she was a city girl and had a bit of class about her. Just what Nancy would like in a sister in law.

Joe had never brought a girl home before and the fact she was coming to lunch on Sunday spoke volumes. Maggie was thrilled that Joe had met someone he cared for and also thought she was a very presentable girl, but the main thing was she made Joe happy. It would also make

John happy to see his son settled. Maggie knew he worried that Joe might end up with a shrew of a wife just as he had worried about Nancy before she married Peter.

Nancy pondered on her situation; if it turned out she could have no more children she decided she would return to work. Mr Jones her old boss at the post office had said she was one of the best workers he had ever had the pleasure of employing, and if ever she wanted to come back he would try his best to fit her in. That was over seven years ago of course and things change. It would be worth asking though.

Elsie would be able to go to her Granny's after school and Peter could leave the pit. Perhaps he could get a nice job selling cars. That market was taking off as more ordinary working class people were able to afford a small motor. They had been having a look around the yards themselves. Nancy could just imagine what people would say if the Martins were the first in the rows to own a car. She remembered the time she had laid wall to wall carpet in her living room. 'Pretentious,' was the word used by a woman in the queue at the co-op. What was pretentious about wanting the house looking nice? wondered Nancy.

Then there was the question of the house, if Peter left the pit they would have to give up number 8 Front Row and find something else, something in the village proper. A nice little cottage in Woodvale Terrace, perhaps, or even farther afield. However that would interfere with Elsie's schooling... With a start Nancy realised she was planning a future that appealed to her, what if the Dr said there was no reason she could not have more children? What plans would she have then?

Picking up a fashion magazine to divert her thoughts she flipped through the pages, until the girl called her name and she rose to enter the doctor's room with more than a little apprehension.

*****

Up by the moor at Mile End, Annie Fell was collecting the eggs. The hens hadn't been laying too well lately, and she hoped they weren't going off.

The money Annie got from selling her eggs helped supplement the wage she got cleaning for the Reverend Dodds up at the Manse. He was an easy man to work for, clean in his habits and not too demanding about meals. He saw to his own breakfast and midday meal then Annie went up and cooked him a hot dinner around about 5pm in the afternoon.

Annie had been widowed about four years now. William, her late husband, ever the conscientious shepherd, had spent nearly a week bringing in the new lambs and pregnant sheep that had been stranded in the hills when an unexpected snow fall had cut them off. Working long hours soaked to the skin had resulted in a bad bout of bronchitis which rapidly turned into pneumonia. It was all over very quickly and Annie found herself left to bring up the three children on her own. Billy, the oldest, was ten at the time, Bobby eight and little Mary only five.

Three months ago, when Billy turned fourteen, he had informed his mother that he was old enough to get a job. He was going down the pit. Annie pleaded with him but like his father before him he was determined to do what he saw as the right thing. The right thing in Billy's mind was to become the man of the house and provide for his mother and the other children, or at least to the best of his ability.

The pit paid the best wages so that is where he went. Annie had to admit that the extra money was a great help, Bobby now had strong shoes for the big school instead of canvas plimsolls, and Billy was insisting she buy new winter coats for Mary and herself. She could really do with one she hadn't had a new stitch of clothing in over five years.

Still and all she hated the idea of her boy going down the shaft every day. Well, the least she could do was make sure there was a hot hearty meal for him when he came off the day shift this afternoon. "He still has the appetite of a growing boy, coupled with that of a working man,

and can put away an inordinate amount of food.'
his mother thought as she set about peeling the
pile of potatoes on the draining board.

*****

Grace, Ellen, and Isobel, had finished
pegging the last of Isobel's sheets. Ellen's load of
nappies and towels were in the rinse water ready
for mangling and Chappies work clothes,
encrusted with coal dust, were steeping in the last
of the hot water in the boiler.
    As the three women stood chatting the
strong aroma of frying came from Maggies open
back door. Old John was having his breakfast.
Grace thought she felt a tremble beneath her feet
and glanced down in puzzlement. Seconds later a
great shudder passed through the green. The
women stared at each other in fright, and then
comprehension dawned.
    "Oh! Jesus, it's the pit" breathed Grace
her face draining of all colour..

*****

She had only just uttered the words when
the pit siren began to wail.
    Dashing inside Grace threw open the
bedroom door, Alex was already struggling into
his clothes. All along the rows, doors were flung

open and men, women, and even children were pouring out and running up the hill to the pit head.

When Grace and Alex came out they found old John struggling along leaning heavily on his cane. "Stay put, John,' said Alex. "My Joes down there," gasped John in anguish. "I know man, but I'll send you word. It may not be too bad." However, Grace remembered what she had felt beneath her feet, and knew it was bad.

Reluctantly John turned back to his front door. Alex murmured to Grace to stay with him and make sure Maggie was okay.

On seeing John turn back Maggie had gone inside and emerged with a kitchen chair. Setting it down on the pavement by the door she returned for a second one for herself.

Grace followed her in, the table held the remains of the fried meal and the still hot teapot. Placing some cups on a tray Grace carried the tea out to the old couple sitting side by side. They were not physically touching but were as united as a husband and wife could be. She was a bit worried about Maggie, her colour was that of wet clay and her hands were shaking. For the first time Grace saw her as an old woman.

Isobel Ford hurried past, her coat pulled tight over her extended belly. 'Of course! Jim was down,' Grace called out to her but she did not hear, or chose not to, just continued to stumble along in her blind panic.

'Who else was down?' Grace wondered, then it struck her. 'Peter Martin! The same Peter who had asked Alex to change shifts. If he had not, Alex would be down there now. Did Alex realize? Of course he did, stupid thought.' her heart ached for her man knowing he would be feeling responsible for Peter's circumstances.

Peter was also in Maggies thoughts, along with Joe, these two were good mates. God willing they would both be safe.

Ellen Chapman joined the little group on the pavement, the two little girls with slices of fruit bread in their hands. Ellen was holding little Nell who was guzzling on her feeding bottle. The siren had frightened her and she had started screaming.

Ellen's first instinct was to make for the pit head but she realized no one would want to listen to a screaming baby, and girls turned whiny at the tension around them, despite having a rare treat of fruit loaf. She was in a quandary, what should she do? How would it look if she did not go up? Grace made the decision for her by telling her to stay with them and Alex would send word as soon as he could.

Inside the wee school the children were very restless. The teachers Mrs Budd and Miss Linden tried to keep them occupied but it was difficult. Alice Tod, with the infants, was coping better although she was very agitated herself. She kept thinking about Joe who was on the day shift.

Joe and Alice had been seeing a lot of each other and since last weekend could be classed as walking out together.

Lunch last Sunday had been with her parents in the city. When she first told them she was seeing a miner her mother Jane had been horrified. She could do better than that. A nice young man in a profession would be more appropriate. It had taken a lot of cajoling on both Alice and her father's part to talk Jane into asking Joe for lunch.

Alan, Alice's father, was a dentist of some repute in the city and had hoped his daughter would make a suitable match. When he saw the light in Alice's eyes as she spoke of Joe he knew that this young man was her choice and therefore, as far as he was concerned more than suitable. At least he felt they had to meet the boy before passing judgement.

The lunch was a pleasant success, Alan found Joe a likeable lad, and they spent some time talking about the skill in extracting teeth and the skill in extracting coal. In the one case care had to be taken not to injure the patient. In the other, equal care had to be exercised to avoid bringing the roof down on top of the workers.

Jane had laid on a spread with salmon sandwiches, cut in neat little triangles, and a variety of cakes from Thompson's bakery. She had to admit that Joe was a nice enough boy and showed more manners than some of the sons of her friends. The afternoon ended in a friendly game of cards with Alan winning most hands and lording it over them in his affable way.

Next Sunday it was Alice's turn to be looked over. Lunch at Maggie's was set for 12 noon, and Alice was a just little bit uneasy. The only contact she'd had with Maggie was a brief good morning after church on Sundays; Joe's sister Nancy was a different story.

Nancy was often up at the school with one complaint or another. She felt that little Elsie was not getting enough attention, or she didn't want Elsie sitting beside that dirty boy Jones. Most of her complaints were not justified but Mrs Budd always listened politely and did her best to smooth things over.

Elsie was a friendly little girl and the teacher did not want her to be disliked by the other children because of her mother. The problem had been discussed in the staff room so Alice was aware of Nancy's reputation. Now she was to have lunch with Joe's parents where his sister and her husband would also be present.

At the moment Sunday lunch was the farthest thing from Alice's mind. When Mrs Budd asked what shift Joe was on and Alice told her he was down this morning she immediately informed Mr O'Brien and arrangements were made for the infants to be split between herself and Miss Linden to allow Alice to go to the pit head.

Mr O'Brien was annoyed with himself for not thinking of this himself, after all the girl lodged with him and his wife and they knew of her attachment to the Wilson boy. Hopefully things were under control and everyone would soon be home safe. Somehow he doubted this, Mr Brown had not yet returned and that did not bode well.

Mr Brown, the janitor had gone up to the pit to find out what he could, and to reassure the mothers there that the children would be taken care of and not allowed out until provisions had been made for them.

Back at the school Mr O'Brien had instructed the dinner ladies to try to stretch the meals to cover the children who usually went home for lunch, they would not get a lot but it would suffice.

*****

The throng at the pit head stood mostly in silence. The few who needed to talk did so in hushed voices. More and more people kept arriving as the news spread over the county.

Doctor Craig had abandoned his morning surgery and come up with Constable Price from the local police station. He would be on standby until the medical team and ambulances on their way from the city arrived. The Salvation Army came with their ever hot urn, and moved quietly among the waiting crowd handing out cups of sweet tea.

In a village often divided by sectarian differences the Reverent Dodds and Father Kelly also went among the fearful crowd waiting for news. All hoping for the best, but dreading the worst.

Local miners on other shifts were now joined by men from collieries all over the county. In all there were literally hundreds of men on standby ready to go down if needed. Only a mining community can understand the horror of what was happening.

Alex, on a line to the pit bottom, had spoken to Andrew Wells, a senior shot-firer. Drew told him fifty three men had made it to the bottom of the shaft. There had been an explosion in number three tunnel but he did not know any more at this stage. Between them Alex and Drew organized for the first lot of men to be brought up. A few had quite bad injuries, but fortunately no fatalities. However there was bad news, six men were unaccounted for.

This is what Alex had been dreading. Fires and falls were one thing, but missing men was something he didn't want to hear. He had assembled the best of his rescue team left above ground and prepared to go down to access the situation.

When Alice reached the crowd she stared in horror. Many of the faces were that of the mothers of her pupils. 'How many men went down in a shift?' She wondered.

Looking round she noticed a young pregnant woman who looked like she was on the verge of collapse. Alice lifted an old wooden box lying by the garden bed near the manager's office. A bed filled with wild primroses, so incongruous in the given situation.

Alice approached the girl and convinced her to sit. Doctor Craig saw her there and came over, he advised her to go down home but Isobel mutely shook her head. A passing sally army man brought two cups of tea, and, to keep the doctor happy, Isobel managed to drink some. There was no way she was leaving here while Jim was still underground. Alice found another box so she could sit beside Isobel and keep an eye on her; it looked as if the baby was due any day.

A deathly silence fell over the crowd as the wheel began to turn, bringing the cage to the surface. Volunteers were ready and waiting to assist the men should they need it.

The miners poured out, black streaked faces shining with sweat and exhaustion. Two were carried by their workmates, one whose leg was clearly broken and an older man who was in a state of collapse.

The ambulance men moved in to relieve the men and transfer the injured to the ambulance.

There were a few more with lacerations and all were having a hard time catching their breath.

The women had held back to let the helpers do their work, then, in a rush those who saw their husbands or sons moved forward to meet and hold their menfolk, but many stood looking in vain.

Isobel saw Jim as he left the cage, even from this distance she could see a large gash across his forehead. As she struggled to rise she found herself restrained by Alice. Someone pointed Jim in the right direction and he dashed to his wife's side. As he hugged her the tears streamed down her face and her body trembled with relief.

Alice looked again at the cage, when she did not see Joe her stomach dropped and her heart raced. 'Be sensible,' she told herself, there are more men waiting to come up. Joe will be among them.

The first ambulance took off with the more serious of the hurt men. Jim refused to go, so Doctor Craig patched him up temporarily. Jim was one of Alex's trained rescue workers, although, it had all been theory up til now. He wanted to stay but as he was already exhausted Alex sent him home with Isobel, assuring him if he was needed he would be sent for. Constable Price bundled both him and Isobel into his car and drove them down home.

Alice stood alone as the cage descended once more, this time containing Alex who was going down to see for himself what could be done.

It was still not known exactly what had happened but Drew Wells had reported that six men were unaccounted for. On reaching the bottom Alex and Drew supervised some more men into the cage and sent it on its way up.

Joe Wilson, Andrew Pyke. Albert Jones, Chappie Chapman, Peter Martin and Billy Fells were not among them.

*****

When the names of the missing were known at the surface, James Long took on the difficult job of telling John and Maggie. James had just come up from hell himself and Enid was there waiting. Suffering only from slight smoke inhalation James was able to walk down the hill leaning lightly on his wife's arm.

As they approached the little group outside number seven, John knew at once that his son was among the missing. He had seen the police car dropping Isobel and Jim at their door and after seeing Isobel safe inside Jim had come over to tell John what he knew. How there had been a major explosion and there were fires burning in pockets in the tunnels. Alex had gone down to assess the situation, and unfortunately there were some missing, but at that stage Jim did not know who.

Jim and Joe were best friends and had been since primary school, they had even started in the pit the same day. When Jim had reached the bottom of the shaft he had looked around at the crowd of anxious men but could not see Joe. That didn't mean he wasn't there he told himself. No need to worry old John and Maggie. Now like John he guessed the bad news James was bringing.

As James told the names, Grace's heart turned over. Among the missing was Maggie's son, Joe, her son-in-law, Peter, and poor Ellen's abusive husband Chappie.

Enid Long looked at the pram containing eight month old Thomas Graham and three month old Nell Chapman. Catching Ellen's eye, she called the two little girls over and told them they were coming for a visit to Auntie Enid's, and pushing the pram she nodded to Grace. Enid Long, one of the few women in the rows who looked down her nose at Ellen, had compassion in her heart.

John had risen and Grace took one arm while Ellen took the other. Maggie told the little group that Nancy was expected back on the four thirty bus. It was agreed that she should stay behind and meet her daughter with the terrible news that both her husband and brother were missing in the mine.

Making their way up the hill the old man and the two women met others coming down. The sympathetic silence said more than words ever could.

The Salvation Army had erected a large tent equipped with chairs. Alice was sitting by herself when Joe's father arrived. He placed his arm round the young girl's shoulders and as they clung together in despair Alice finally gave in and let the tears she had been holding back flow from her eyes

Grace went up to the table and got a cup of tea for Ellen, who felt that tea was coming out her ears but knew it was a kindly gesture from someone who didn't know what else to do.

The families of Andrew Pyke and Albert Jones were sitting in a huddle, the two men were from a village five miles south and many of their friends who worked in other pits were among the men involved in the rescue.

Sitting in the circle of her sister's arms Annie Fell shuddered with emotion while her twelve year old Bobby stood stony faced at her shoulder.

*****

After the second cage went up Alex and Drew began their exploration of the tunnels. At first the smoke was not too bad but as they went deeper in they found more pockets of fire. At the heading of tunnel four they were driven back by the acrid fumes and increased smoke. Alex, realizing the seriousness of the situation, sent word to the top that there was no hope of farther exploratory work without the use of breathing apparatus.

Drew went to the surface with instructions to send Bill Calder down with the two asbestos fire fighting suits and the breathing gear. Drew had been down since the start of shift at 5:00am that morning, it was now after 5:00pm and Alex insisted he take a break. Bill was a capable man and Alex had confidence in him as a trained member of his team.

Wearing the protective gear the two men attempted to follow the rail tracks along past the entrance to number four. They knew the air would only last an hour so they had to find out as much as possible in that time. There had been a few falls but the fires were the big problem. There was a lot of fire damp about and spontaneous fires were breaking out when this ignited.

The one positive hope was that the fires seemed to be in tunnels three and four, and the missing men had been working in tunnel number six. However Alex knew that until the fires were quelled there was no hope of reaching number six.

Equipped with goggles and breathing masks, the first team descended to the bottom. The sumps were going full blast as the water was relayed to the areas where the flames were the worst. On the surface water had been diverted from the village mains and pumped down in gallons.

For over twenty hours the three teams of men fought the heat and smoke, taking it in turns to spell each other. All except Alex and Bill, they stayed down the whole time. At some point during the long night they had managed to reach the heading of tunnel six.

A few yards in there had been a massive fall. This could mean one of several things. The men had been caught under the cave in, or they could be trapped behind it. If trapped behind there was a slim chance they had found a pocket of air and had survived. Or, as was sadly more likely, the deadly fumes and gas would have ended their lives.

The last team before they broke through the final fall, included Jim Ford, and Drew Wells, both of whom had returned to help after a short rest.

On the surface, the rescue teams, officials and volunteers, along with the families and friends of the missing miners still waited with desperate hope that the men would be found safe.

The newspaper reporters had arrived but with great respect did not intrude on the anxiety of the people waiting.

John still sat with stoic bearing, while Maggie had surrendered to lying on a makeshift bunk staring into nothingness. Her meeting with Nancy from the bus had been all she feared.

Nancy's visit to the specialist, although inconclusive, was promising. The examination had been very uncomfortable and the questions had caused Nancy some embarrassment.

The upshot was that Doctor Melville thought there may have been some trauma at the time of Elsie's birth but would need farther tests to confirm this. It would mean a day or two in hospital, but, if it was as the doctor suspected, a minor operation would fix things and Nancy could have as many babies as she wished.

This had set her to worrying, people would want to know what was wrong if it became known she was in hospital and she did not want it to be public knowledge she was seeking advice on her fertility. Still it sounded like good news and Jim would be over the moon.

As Nancy left the hospital in fairly high spirits and headed down Rimmer Street to Thompson's tea rooms situated above the famous bakery she failed to notice the ambulance men carrying the wounded miners into the emergency department.

After a warming cuppa and a luscious cream cake she wandered around the shops gazing at baby clothes on display in the smarter stores. When Elsie was born there had not been much of a choice and it was pleasing to see the beautiful things that were available these days.

All going well Maggie would be getting the knitting needles out before too long.

Still on cloud nine she boarded the bus heading back home thinking all the time what the future might hold.

When the bus passed through an unnaturally quite village and drew up at the stop at the foot of the rows Nancy rose to alight and saw her mother waiting at the bus stop. One look at Maggie's face told her something dreadful had happened. Immediately her heart started pounding, where was Elsie? Had something happened to her? Or was it dad?

The bus drew away and Maggie took hold of her daughter's arm. In a flat dull voice she told her the frightening news of her husband and brother.

Nancy's legs gave way as everything went black and she slid slowly to the ground. James Long who had been watching Maggie from his window across the street rushed over and helped her to her feet. Saying nothing, he placed his arm around her shoulders, and taking Maggie on the other side, he walked mother and daughter up the hill, back to the pithead.

Now, as Maggie rested quietly on a makeshift bed Nancy sat like her father, putting on as brave a face as she could manage. There could be no repeat of the incident at the bus stop; she must be in complete control, she told herself.

*****

The task facing the men at the entrance to number six was enormous. The fall had been significant and had sealed the heading completely. Alex sent word back for props to be brought in and they started to clear the way. It was a delicate task, one wrong move could bring the whole lot down on top of them. "Make haste slowly" was the order of the day.

It was Jim Ford who made the first breakthrough, a small hole that was quickly shored up as the men worked to enlarge it. When it was of a size to allow access they moved in one at a time.

Alex was first through and his worse fears were confirmed. About sixteen feet in lay the still bodies of their six workmates. Joe and Peter sat with their backs to the wall, their right hands in a handshake that showed the respect and friendship these men had for each other. Albert and Andrew lay stretched out face down, each had removed his shirt and covered his head. Chappie Chapman had both arms tightly locked around young Billy Fells, the boy's head resting on Chappie's rough flannel shirt front. Chappie's head had fallen forward and his lips were brushing the top of the young boy's hair.

They had all perished from the effects of the poisonous gasses. There was not a blemish on them.

Jim Ford fell to his knees and sobbed like a baby.

Alex contacted the engine room for stretchers and relayed word to the surface to have the ambulances standing by. The rescue team was bringing the fallen men out.

In the tent the reverend Mr Dodds, accompanied by the mine manager and an official from the recently formed coal board, broke the news to the small group huddled around John Wilson.

Annie Fells collapsed in a sobbing heap and Doctor Craig gave her an injection to help her through this dreadful time. She had never lost faith that her son would be saved. Young Bobby who had tried so hard to be strong for his mother, forgot to be brave and became again the child he was, and wept for his brother.

The rest of the families had, in all truth given up hope. Grace who had spent the last twenty four hours going between home and the pit head, put her arms round Ellen and led her out of the tent to wait at the top of the shaft for the cage coming up.

Alice's father had come from the city to be with his daughter. Standing here now Alan couldn't help but wonder 'if people had any idea, as they sit in comfort by their blazing fires, what these men went through to make it possible.'

Nancy and John with Maggie between them followed the others out and they all stood in silence as the wheel started to turn, bringing six brave men to the surface for the last time.

*****

Three ambulances were waiting, one to take Andrew and Albert the five miles to their home village and the other two to transport the four local men to the miner's welfare hall in on the west side of the village. Preparations had been made to turn the hall into a temporary mortuary.

This is the hall where the miners played dominos and draughts, card games and pool while sharing a beer with mates. Where they had Saturday night sing songs, and held social dances. It was where the children had their Christmas party, and a gala on the first of May. The youth had their amateur boxing and the local pigeon fanciers held their meetings. Weddings, and yes, funeral teas. In fact all things pertaining to village life went on in this hall.

And now a Mortuary.

The co-op provided the trestles and boards to lay out the bodies. Women from all over the rows came with pails of warm water, clothes and towels. When the ambulance men had lain the men on the boards their women folk came forward to do the cleansing.

As Maggie stood by her son she became aware of Alice at her side. The girl's eyes were red and held a haunted empty look. Dipping her hands in the water Maggie squeezed out a soft flannel and handed it to Alice then together his mother and the girl who would have been his wife proceeded to wash Joe's body.

Annie's sister Jenny was on hand to care for the nephew she had helped bring into the world fourteen years ago. Her pain for her sister was a tangible thing. She had watched as Annie struggled bravely with William's death but would she survive the cruelty of this savage blow, it was enough to break your heart.

Ellen's new friend Enid stood by her side as they gazed down on Chappie. Ellen had long since ceased to love this man but she could still remember the lad she had been enthralled with when she was young and starry eyed. She would never have wished to see him like this.

As Ellen's memories rolled back the years she realised someone else was standing gazing on Chappie. Others watched as Annie Fells lifted his, as yet, unwashed hand and pressed it to her lips. "God bless you laddie" she murmured. In the eyes of many Chappie Chapman had redeemed himself. Ellen's children would remember their father as the man who had comforted young Billy Fells in his last frightening hours.

Unsure how she would be received, Grace approached Nancy, who, with a grateful nod handed her a flannel cloth. Nancy herself was using a large sea sponge of such delicate softness, one which she had purchased that day in town in the hope it would be needed for a new baby. Never had she dreamed it would be put to the use of something so terrible as washing the still body of her beloved husband. Now she would never be able to tell Peter that their dreams of having a son might really have happened.

****

The whole town turned out the morning of the funeral. The schools remained closed as did every shop in the village.

Farmer McKenzie, with the help of his farmhands, had spread straw all the way from the rows to the cemetery. There were no horse drawn carriages with iron wheels to muffle but this mark of respect from the farming community was recognised by the villagers.

Alice came with her parents Alan and Jane. She had returned to the city the day after the men were brought up. Jane had never seen her daughter look so sad, her heart ached for the young girl, and though she could not imagine the pain of the families who had lost their men what she did feel was hard enough to bear.

Two young soldiers on compassionate leave stood to attention as their older brother's coffin was lowered down.

It was ironic that the cemetery was situated above the workings of the very pit where the men had died.

Many officials and politicians from the local, and county councils were there. The government and national coal board were also represented.

The three men were buried in graves side by side. The boy, Billy Fells, went in beside his father, leading Annie to think that when her time came to join them he would be tucked safe between them just as he had been when, as a toddler, he would squeeze in beside them in their old feather bed.

The service was taken by both the Reverend Dodds and Father Kelly. All sectarian differences forgotten as a village mourned.

One person was not at the cemetery. Isobel Ford had been delivered of a fine healthy son in the early hours of the morning. The joy of his son was marred by the sad proceedings now taking place, and Jim knew that every birthday his boy had would bring back the anguish of this week. Isobel looked at it differently, she explained to Jim that the baby was like a monument to his friends and as such was a remembrance to be thankful for. He could see the truth in her words.

That evening as the sun dropped behind the hill on which the pit head stood Grace wondered how long it would take the village to heal.

Ten Years Later
****

Nancy
*****

After the funeral the county council had offered the widows a council house on the new estate being built to the west of the village. Nancy had a very pretty three bedroom place, everywhere, except the kitchen, boasted wall to wall carpets.

Maggie had come to stay when John died and was now an old lady in her seventies. She found Nancy's house very comfortable with all the modern conveniences, and Elsie was still as charming company as ever. Maggie still had a stubborn streak of independence and insisted on helping with the housework. After all how hard could it be for a woman who had beaten rugs over a fence and scrubbed clothes on a washboard, to run the vacuum cleaner over the carpets or turn on the new fangled automatic washing machine.

Nancy had returned to work; Mr Jones was as good as his word and had soon found a place for her. She was now the manageress of a large branch which had opened in the new town being built fifteen miles to the east. She was the first woman from the rows to pass her driving test, and now owned a smart little blue car. She had many of the things she thought about that day, sitting in the hospital waiting room. She would give them all up if she could just have Peter back.

Elsie was now a young lady of eighteen, working in an exclusive leather goods store in the city. Her training included accompanying the elderly owner on buying trips with the view of her becoming the main buyer and taking over from her boss in the near future. Yes a daughter to be proud of.

Ellen
*****

Ellen had been given a four bedroom place; it was comfortable like Nancy's although not so 'pretentious.' Best of all Ellen loved her twin tub. Leaning over the wash board and struggling with the huge mangle was only a memory now.

The three youngest girls Lizzy, Jenny, and Nelly, had the big front room. For some years one big double bed had held all three girls but more recently a single bed had been bought for Nelly.

Lizzy and Jenny, were 'Irish Twins,' both born in the same year, one at the beginning and one at the end. They had always been very dependent on each other and inclined to be nervy. Ellen wondered if it went back to the day their father died and their mother seemed to have deserted them. However at twelve and thirteen they had recently joined the guides and their confidence seemed to be growing. They loved to visit their Auntie Enid who had a soft spot for them and spoiled them rotten.

Dick and David, who shared the largest of the back rooms, were a different story, both good looking boys in the Chapman tradition. Dick at sixteen was already turning the girl's heads, and David would not be far behind. Ellen didn't worry too much about them they were good boys and with their mothers encouragement determined to do well.

Dick was serving an apprenticeship as a motor mechanic and couldn't wait to get his licence. David's head teacher had advised Ellen to let him stay on to take his highers. He had university potential, and, much to Ellen's relief, neither would ever have to go near a pit.

Agnes worked in the local grocery store and was walking out with Robert Graham, eldest son of Grace and Alex. If Agnes recalled how her father was not all he should have been she never mentioned it. Like her mother she kept her own counsel. Ellen had no worries about Agnes.

All in all Ellen was happy with her life, especially since Brian Cook had come into it. Brian had been in the army with Chappie's younger brothers and had visited with them when they were home on leave. Two years ago he had left the army and settled in the village. He opened a small repair garage which was steadily growing. It was to Brian that Dick was apprenticed. He treated Ellen with a respect and tenderness she had never known and she glowed as their friendship grew into a gentle love.

Annie
*****

Up at Mile End Annie spent her time caring for any stray cats or dogs that came her way. Not only cats and dogs but any hurt or lost animal. She had a way with them. She had turned down the house offered by the council preferring to stay in the home she had known with her husband and family. Some said she was a bit touched but most village people remembered and understood. She still did a bit of cleaning for the reverend Dodds and farmer McKenzie, although it was more out of the goodness of their hearts that they kept her on.

Much like Ellen in the old days, the villagers kept an eye on Annie. Bobby had done well for himself at school and was now well on his way to being an architect. He had his own flat in the city. His future looked bright but he would never forget what he owed to his brother and hoped Billy would have been proud of him.

Young Mary had a position in the wages office at the car factory. She still lived at home but had recently acquired her licence and a small car, making it easier for her to get out and about. Mary also knew that her mother was more capable than most people thought; Annie just wanted to be left in peace.

Grace
*****

Grace carefully wrapped the little china teapot that had sat on the mantle shelf for the last fifteen years. It was added to the box holding her best china. No removal men were allowed to touch these precious things. While her hands were busy with the packing Grace let her mind wander back through the years.

For the most part she had been happy in this house, they had come here when Robert was five and Eddie was on the way. Now Robert was twenty and stepping out with Agnes Chapman, and Eddie was a big hulk of a boy of fifteen. Thomas, her baby, had also been born here. He hated when she referred to him as her baby, so she did not do it very often, usually only to tease him. But in her heart that is how she would always see him. He was off with his friends on their bikes, up the pit road more than likely.

The pit was closed now. While many had lamented over the closure Grace was secretly relieved. She had long wished that Alex would find another job away from the pit but never voiced it to him. She knew that somehow he felt an obligation to the men who had died, especially

Peter. Now, along with many other redundant miners, he travelled to the car factory that had been established near the new town.

The rows were due to come down now. Everyone had been allocated a council house. Many chose to go to the new town but Grace and Alex opted for the same scheme where Ellen and Nancy lived.

Grace's mind went back to the drying green on that fateful day. Ellen's clothes had lain in the rinse water for three days before someone discovered them. Chappie's work things still in the scummy water in the boiler were quietly disposed of. Isobel's sheets and Grace's own wash had been taken down by neighbours, and returned folded and ironed.

Grace lifted the letter with the Australian postmark from the sideboard. Inside was a photograph of two young boys and a baby girl. The boys were swinging on an old car tyre hanging from a tree limb by a sturdy rope. The eldest, who had his birthday last week, was grinning from ear to ear. Grace wondered if Joseph Peter William Ford knew how he got his name.

Jim never again went near the pit after the terrible days of the unsuccessful rescue. Within six months, with Isobel and their baby son, he was on his way to Western Australia. They settled in the south west no to far from the coast. Many of the pictures Isobel had sent to Grace showed them on the beach. Jim was happy she wrote. It had proved the best thing to get right away. Perhaps some day when the children were older they might manage a trip back.

Last week the village held a memorial for the men lost ten years ago. At the service Grace had seen Alice sitting with her father, an older more mature Alice. It turned out she had also gone to Australia after Joe's death, and now taught at a primary school in Kalgoorlie. Among her pupils, many were the children of miners. Alice had made the long journey back to be at the memorial and visit with her parents. When Grace told her that Isobel and Jim were in the south west of the same state she promised to look them up in the school holidays.

As Grace cleared the items from the drawer in the sideboard her hand came in contact with a small square velvet box. Opening the box she gazed on the medal presented to Alex in recognition of the part he played in the attempted rescue and recovery of the trapped men. Alex had accepted it gracefully, brought it home, and placed it in this drawer where it had remained unopened for the last ten years.

Closing the box Grace dropped it in with all the other bits and bobs and with a sigh continued packing for the move to their new home.

The End

Made in United States
Orlando, FL
01 December 2024

54351943R00032